Finding the Wor

Finding the Words is a book of 42 worksheets for photocopying, designed p... help students improve reading and vocabulary skills. Each worksheet contains a piece of reading matter which is used as a basis for a variety of vocabulary, 'filling the gaps' and 'cloze' exercises. The worksheets encourage students to think carefully about what they read, whether it is for practical everyday purposes or for pleasure. All of the worksheets provide practice in the many skills required for getting the most out of reading and, in some, opportunities for writing and discussion are also given.

The Contents are arranged in alphabetical order of title. It is left to tutors and students to choose which worksheets to tackle, according to their particular interests, vocabulary and reading ability. The Index *(p. 48)* gives more detailed guidance to the kinds of exercise and the topics covered.

Lists of the original words omitted from the text of 'cloze' and other exercises are included *(pp. 46 & 47)*. We must emphasise strongly that they have been provided solely for the interest of users of the worksheets and they should not, under any circumstances, be regarded as the correct words. Indeed, in many cases, students will be able to think of much more suitable words to fit the context than those in the original text.

Answers are given for the questions in *It can't be true (1) & (2) (pp. 20 & 21)* and in *World Records (p. 45)*, to save students having to search for them in reference books - although this should not deter them from doing so!

Finding the Words should prove useful for work related to NVQ Key Skills, National Curriculum (English) and City & Guilds & SCOTVEC Wordpower Certificates.

Please read the copyright / photocopying restrictions below.

COPYRIGHT / PHOTOCOPYING RESTRICTIONS
Purchasers may photocopy *Finding the Words* for use <u>within their own centre or single college/school site</u>. We ask you to respect this permission and not to allow copies to be transferred to other colleges, schools, sites or centres. A tutor who purchases a personal copy may use *Finding the Words* on more than one site, provided that they restrict its use to the classes they personally teach and do not allow copies to be passed to other tutors and students. Items from *Finding the Words* may not be reproduced in magazines, newsletters, books or on computer disk/tape without the prior permission of the publishers.

Publishers: Brown and Brown,
Keeper's Cottage,
Westward,
Wigton
Cumbria CA7 8NQ
Tel. 016973 42915

Copyright © Hugh and Margaret Brown 1998

All rights reserved.

Photocopying is permitted subject to the restrictions detailed on page 1.

If you would like to receive our catalogue of publications for teaching reading, spelling, writing and basic maths, please contact:
Brown and Brown Publishing, Keeper's Cottage, Westward, Wigton, Cumbria CA7 8NQ
Tel. 016973 42915

First published 1998
Reprinted 2000, 2002

ISBN 1 870596 69 2

Printed by Reed's Ltd., Penrith, Cumbria on 100% recycled paper and card.

Contents

*All titles beginning with the indefinite article (**a**) and the definite article (**the**) are grouped together.*

A Breath of Fresh Air	4	Safe and sound	33
A Deaf Ear (1)	5	Signs and Notices (1)	34
A Deaf Ear (2)	6	Signs and Notices (2)	35
A Great Meal	7	Signs and Notices (3)	36
Beware of pickpockets	8	Signs and Notices (4)	37
Blackpool Pleasure Beach	9	That takes the biscuit !	38
Come up and see me	10	The Blizzard	39
Crimes that went wrong (1)	11	The Day of the Exam	40
Crimes that went wrong (2)	12	The Great Canadian Ice Storm	41
Dropping a line (1)	13	The Modern Wedding	42
Dropping a line (2)	14	The Sad Tale of Mr. Goodyear	43
Food scares	15	The War-time Volunteer	44
Fox-hunting - for or against ?	16	World Records	45
Get a life!	17	*Words omitted from the texts*	46
Having a good chat	18	*Index*	48
Hero or villain ?	19		
It can't be true (1)	20		
It can't be true (2)	21		
My Best Shot	22		
On tap	23		
Out for a duck	24		
Race of a lifetime	25		
Reading Instructions (1)	26		
Reading Instructions (2)	27		
Reading Instructions (3)	28		
Reading Instructions (4)	29		
Reading Instructions (5)	30		
Reading Instructions (6)	31		
Reading Instructions (7)	32		

A Breath of Fresh Air

Choose a word from the box to fit each gap in the article.

It is hard to imagine a country with no countryside; a country covered _____ with buildings and roads. Even people who prefer the _____ and excitement of city life may sometimes feel _____ by the hard landscape in which they _____ and work.

Everybody wants and needs _____ bit of 'countryside' - a plant in the office, a _____ box, a garden for the kids to play in or an allotment _____ growing food. Townies who, on holiday, can't sleep for the _____ and are terrified of cows, would miss their game of _____ in the local park. And how would they survive without the trees which line their hot, traffic-choked streets, absorbing _____ and providing welcome summer shade?

_____ towns and cities in the U.K. have a protective green belt around them - a _____ against the developers which prevents built-up _____ melting, like butter, into each other. These days, _____ is much talk of 'green field' and 'brown field' sites, _____ the Government tries to balance the need for more _____ - and the schools, hospitals, shops and other facilities that _____ along with it - against the need for open spaces.

_____ everyone wants to go in for 'the good life' and _____ live in the country but, without the green spaces, _____ would we go for a breath of fresh air?

has	exactly	bustle	live	there	football
arenas	window	were	buffet	silence
pollution	cricket	four	most	actually
areas	overpowered	their	as	housing	go
life	for	buffer	not	where	entirely

A Deaf Ear (1)

Choose words from the box to fill the gaps in this story.

A Somerset man had been _____ in one ear since the age of three. Many _____ later, he was visiting a _____ doctor who _____ to have a look at the deaf _____ . The doctor, to her amazement, _____ that there was a small cork _____ the ear. The man took the news quite calmly.

"Well, fancy that !" he _____ . "I must have _____ it in there when I was a lad !"

ear	new	inside
put	deaf	found
years	said	asked

A Deaf Ear (2)

Read this story, then do the exercise below.

A woman from Nottingham went to the doctor to complain that she was going deaf. He told her that she needed to have her ears syringed. As he did it, he was amazed to find a baby's tooth inside one ear. It had been stuck there for 30 years !

When she was about five, she lost a tooth. She put it under her pillow, hoping that the tooth fairy would find it and leave her a sixpence. After she fell asleep, the tooth got into her ear and stayed there for thirty years. It had never caused her any pain at all !

Fill in the gaps in the story with different words from the ones used above.

A woman from Nottingham went to the doctor to _____ that she was _____ deaf. He told her that she _____ to have her ears syringed. As he did it, he was _____ to find a baby's tooth inside one ear. It had been _____ there for 30 years !

When she was _____ five, she lost a tooth. She put it _____ her pillow, _____ that the tooth fairy _____ find it and leave her a sixpence. After she fell asleep, the tooth got _____ her ear and _____ there for thirty years. It had never _____ her any pain at all !

A Great Meal

Read this piece and then do the exercises.

Last night, we went out for a great meal. We went to that pub, *The Great Western*, off the Dock Road. It's great, now that it's been done up. There's a great big bar and a great new dining-room at the back. You can have bar meals or eat in the dining-room and it's great because it's all the same price. All the main meals are only about £6 or £7 and you get great big portions.

The pub has a great choice of beers and it has a really great atmosphere. Another great thing is the choice of sweets. They are all the same price, £2.75, and they have a great choice. I had this great big piece of chocolate cake, with cream. It was called 'Death by Chocolate'. It was great !

1. How many times is the word **great** used in this piece ?

2. Replace all the **greats** with other words. Try not to use any word more than once.

3. Make up a short piece of your own, using one of the expressions below as many times as you can:

   a. nice

   b. brilliant

   c. really really

   d. you know

   e. like

Brown and Brown / Finding the Words

Beware of pickpockets

A. Fill in the gaps in this story. All the missing words are verbs.

Some years ago, a Western businessman was working in Japan. Other people at work _____ him about the thieves on the Tokyo underground system. Some pickpockets would _____ to steal a wallet just as the doors of the train were closing. The victim would be _____ on the train, while the pickpocket was left on the platform.

One morning, the Western businessman _____ the train as usual. Shortly afterwards, he felt a man bump into him. The businessman _____ the warning about pickpockets and felt for his wallet. It had _____ ! He looked up to see the man who had bumped into him leaving the train. The doors began to _____ .

Quickly, the businessman caught hold of the man's coat. The coat was not fastened and the doors _____ on the coat with the businessman holding on to the back of it. The train began to _____ away. The businessman hung on, while the other man was _____ to run alongside the train. In a panic, the man grabbed at a pillar and _____ on to it. His coat was ripped in half. As the train _____ into the tunnel, the businessman thought that, at least, he _____ given the pickpocket a fright as well as ruining his coat.

When he _____ at his office, the businessman telephoned his wife at home, so that she _____ look up the details of his credit cards. He _____ to report their theft to the bank.

"Oh !" she _____ . "I'm glad you've rung. Did you _____ that you left your wallet in the bedroom when you _____ off to work this morning ?"

B. Explain what a verb is.

C. Pick out 5 verbs from the story (apart from the missing ones) **which are made of two or more words.**

   e.g. gave up; had been; was going in; went out

The Tokyo Underground

Blackpool Pleasure Beach

Choose a phrase from the box to fit each gap in the article.

A visit to Blackpool Pleasure Beach is just _____ . It's Britain's most popular tourist attraction and it's an experience not to be missed. Whether you're just out of nappies or just _____ , you'll love it, whatever your age. With over 145 rides, attractions, shops and shows, it has _____ .

For those who've _____ , there's the tallest and fastest roller coaster in the world - 235 feet high, speeds of up to 87 mph and over one mile of twisting and turning track. And there are 9 more roller coasters to choose from too - the _____ choice anywhere in Europe. On top of all that, there's the _____ Play Station which catapults you into the air at 80 mph and then brings you back in an incredible free fall descent.

If you would give _____ , why not take a gentle cruise in the River Caves ? For _____ , take a trip on the overhead Monorail Train. If _____ , try the Tunnel of Love. And if you're the sort who thinks they've _____ , a stroll through Ripley's *Believe It or Not! Odditorium* will have you rubbing your eyes in amazement.

Younger visitors will have _____ galore in Beaver Creek Children's Theme Park. They can get _____ on the white water rapids of the Log Flume and test their driving skills on Bradley's Adventure Car Ride.

If you fancy _____ there are over 45 places to choose from, plus a host of unique shops, a Casino and a Chinese Puzzle Maze. _____ , there are over 9 spectacular live shows throughout the season.

Blackpool Pleasure Beach is more than a day out, it's _____ .

thrills and spills	soaked to the skin	a bite to eat
to crown it all	something for everyone	seen it all before
biggest and best	got the bottle	the holiday of a lifetime
romance is in the air	a bird's-eye view	anything for a quiet life
young at heart	out of this world	stomach-churning

Come up and see me

Read the article, then do the exercise below.

The film star, Mae West, was best known for her one-line remarks. Her famous catch-phrase was "Come up and see me sometime," - a shortened version of a line from her film, *She Done Him Wrong*.

Mae West in
She Done Him Wrong

Mae West was still making films when she was very old. When she was 89 years old, she had a part in the film *Sextette*. Unfortunately, she could no longer remember her lines very well and often got confused by last-minute changes in the script.

The director, Ken Hughes, hit on the idea of putting a small radio receiver in her wig so that he could tell her the lines just before she had to say them. This worked well until, one day, during a love scene, a police helicopter tuned into the same wavelength as the receiver. As a result, Miss West came out with the line, "Traffic on the Hollywood freeway is bogged down."

Despite these problems, Mae West still had a lot of admirers and hangers-on, many of whom tried to tell her the things they thought she wanted to hear. One of these admirers said to her,

"Miss West, you are still so beautiful. You don't look a day over 29."

"Thanks, feller," she replied. "I'm supposed to be 26."

Here are some of Mae West's one-liners. Fill in the missing words.

1. "It's not the men in my life that counts, it's the life in my _____ ."

2. "When I'm good, I'm very, very good, but when I'm _____ , I'm better."

3. "I used to be Snow _____ .... but I drifted."

4. "Between two evils, I always pick the one I haven't _____ before."

5. "A man in the house is _____ two in the street."

6. "It's better to be looked _____ than overlooked."

7. "To err is human, _____ it feels divine."

8. "Marriage is a great institution, but I'm not _____ for an institution yet."

Crimes that went wrong (1)

The Big Mistake

Choose a word from the box to fill each gap in the story.

the	by	with	a
over	out	in	off
and	her	who	to

One night in Los Angeles, Mrs. Sharpe was _____ walking her dog. She was attacked _____ a mugger _____ pushed her _____ the ground _____ forced her to hand _____ her bag.

Unfortunately for _____ mugger, what he made _____ with was not worth _____ lot. _____ bag contained a small shovel and a plastic carrier _____ the dog's droppings _____ it!

Crimes that went wrong (2)

The Big Bang

A. Fill in the gaps in this story. All the missing words are nouns.

In a town called Vang, in Norway, a _____ of expert thieves planned a robbery in great detail. On the _____ of the raid, at the premises of a large local _____ , everything went according to plan.

They broke into the building and found the safe. Then _____ set up an explosive charge that would just blow the _____ off the safe so that they could get out the _____ . After setting the fuse, they ran into the next room, took cover behind a _____ and waited for the explosion.

It came a few _____ later. The safe door was blown off. So was the roof. So were the windows, doors and some of the _____ as the whole building collapsed. The robbers were trapped in the _____ and were arrested by the police soon afterwards.

The one _____ that the thieves had got wrong was that there wasn't any money in the _____ . It had been filled with dynamite !

B. Explain what a noun is.

C. Pick out 5 nouns from the story *(apart from the missing ones)*.

Dropping a line (1)

A. *All these sentences are taken from everyday letters.*

Choose words from the box to fill the gaps.

1. Thank you for your _____ of June 23rd.

2. Please _____ enclosed a copy of my order form and a cheque for £31.48.

3. I am writing to _____ you of my change of address.

4. We were very _____ to hear from Bill yesterday that Mary has died.

5. We _____ for any inconvenience this may have caused.

6. We can assure you that all the information will be kept strictly _____ .

7. Please let me know as soon as possible if you are interested in _____ as places are strictly limited.

8. I am sorry that I have taken so long to _____ to your letter but I have only just returned from holiday.

| attending | sorry | reply | apologise |
| confidential | inform | find | letter |

B. *Which of these words would fit any of the gaps just as well as the words in the box?*

| sad | respond | memo | note | tell |
| private | pleased | going | ask | answer |

Dropping a line (2)

All these sentences are taken from everyday letters.
Fill in the missing words.

1. We are delighted to inform you that you have been _____ to take part in our prize _____ and you could win £1,000,000 !

2. If you have any _____ about this matter, please contact the office given at the top of this letter, quoting your _____ number.

3. I enclose a _____ of our current price list and we look forward to _____ from you in due course.

4. If you do not wish to _____ your membership, please inform the Membership Secretary as soon as _____ .

5. Thank you for the _____ invitation to your daughter's wedding on August 24th, which we are delighted to _____ .

6. The above Policy falls _____ for renewal on 3rd April and we now _____ with details of this year's renewal terms.

7. The Bank _____ that it is unable to extend your overdraft arrangements and _____ you to recommence repayments immediately, as agreed.

8. We can offer you an extremely competitive _____ for your advertising, bearing in mind that we have a _____ of 36,000 copies for each issue.

Food scares

Every tenth word is missing from this article. Fill in the missing words.

Is our food really safe to eat? In the _____ couple of decades, news stories about food safety have _____ on the increase. Hardly a month goes by without _____ new warning or piece of advice from the experts.

_____ of food poisoning are always in the news. There _____ the 'salmonella in eggs' scare in 1988 and there _____ warnings about listeria in 1989 and 1990. Even more _____ was the E. coli outbreak in Scotland in 1996 which _____ in 18 deaths. There have been further cases since. _____ food scares have been about pesticides on and in _____ and vegetables; poisons in shellfish; and chemicals in baby _____ .

The biggest story of all in the U.K. has _____ the BSE, or 'mad cow', crisis. For some years, _____ one took any action on the evidence that began _____ emerge about 'mad cow' disease. Then attempts were made _____ stop BSE occurring in cattle. The public was told _____ was no risk to human health. Some time later, _____ took place in the way beef was slaughtered. Later _____ , there was an announcement that there *could* be a _____ to human health from infected beef and that certain _____ of meat should be avoided. The export of British _____ was banned. The sale of beef on the bone _____ banned and the safety of lamb was questioned. Most _____ consumers seem to have decided to ignore the risks _____ meat sales have begun to return to almost the _____ level as before.

Much food poisoning is caused by _____ way food is prepared and eaten nowadays. More pre-cooked _____ , 'fast food' and frozen food is bought and it _____ often heated quickly in a microwave. Many microwave ovens _____ not heat food evenly and there is a danger _____ ready-made meals are not heated right through.

So _____ can we do to avoid all these dangers? The _____ is that we can't avoid them - but we can _____ down on the risk. Food hygiene is very important _____ our own homes. For example, fresh meat should not _____ stored next to cooked meat; chilled food should be _____ really chilled and hot food must be cooked until _____ is really hot. Food should not be left lying _____ in warm rooms.

Finally, the experts all agree that _____ most important thing is to eat healthy foods - fresh _____ and vegetables, washed and peeled; plenty of fibre and _____ (bread, pasta, rice etc.); less sugar and fewer fatty _____ .

Fox-hunting - for or against ?

Read the arguments for and against fox-hunting, then do the exercise below.

FOR

Fox-hunting has been going on for hundreds of years in the country and it shouldn't be banned just because people in towns don't understand it. Foxes are vicious killers. They kill lambs, sheep, chickens, turkeys and other animals at random. They don't kill them just for food - a fox will bite the heads off 10 or 12 chickens without eating any of them.

The hunt maintains a balance in nature. It keeps fox numbers down in a humane way. The fox is usually killed almost instantly by the dogs. If there were no hunting, farmers would have to resort to shooting or using poisons. Both methods result in a far more painful death for the fox and danger to other wildlife.

AGAINST

Fox-hunting shouldn't be allowed in this day and age. Chasing after a fox with a pack of hounds and encouraging the dogs to catch it and tear it apart with their teeth is barbaric. You can't call it a sport. It is not an effective way of controlling foxes, since the huntsmen always make sure that there are enough foxes left for the 'thrill of the chase'. They could be controlled in a more humane way by shooting them or by the use of poisons.

The people who take part in fox-hunting are not sportsmen. They are blood-thirsty murderers who breed dogs especially to kill other animals. Foxes are beautiful animals. They should be allowed to exist as part of the balance of nature.

What do you think ?   *Complete these sentences, giving your views.*

1. I think that fox-hunting ....

2. The most important thing to remember is that foxes are ....

   ....

3. Country people ....

   .... townies.

4. Killing foxes ....

   ....

Get a life !

Read this article and then do the exercises.

I am one of that rare breed of women - the housewife. Despite the fact that everyone else thinks I should go out and get a job, I am perfectly happy to stay at home looking after the house and the family. I know I'm lucky because we can get by on what my husband earns although, God knows, we could do with a bit more money coming in. Now that the kids are getting older, it gets harder and harder to get them all the clothes and things they need for school.

My sister can't understand why I don't get bored but, when I look at her, I think I get the better deal. We haven't got as much money as them but she gets so worn out rushing out to work, getting child care organised, getting meals for her family and generally getting herself ready for a nervous breakdown.

I've got myself quite well organised. I get up at about 6.30 and get breakfast ready for all the family. My husband gets off to work by 7.30 and it takes me the next half-hour to get the kids out of bed and down for breakfast. We have to get out of the house by 8.20 to get to the Infants' school on time.

On my way home, I often get some shopping and then I get going on the housework - washing, cleaning ironing. It never seems to end.

I get my lunch at about 12.30 and, in the afternoons, I often go and get some more shopping or library books for my grandmother who is housebound. At 3.15, I have to get to the school to meet the kids and then I have to get tea ready for everyone. I do get to a keep-fit class once a week and Neil and I get out at least one evening a week when my mum baby-sits. One day, I'd like to get to college and get a bit more education but I'm not sure I've got the time for it at the moment.

1. How many times does the writer use the words *get*, *gets*, *getting* or *got* ?

2. Re-write the article, changing it so that no '*get*' words are included, if possible. Replace the '*get*' words with as many different words as you can.

3. Write an article from her sister's point of view, explaining why she works and doesn't stay at home.

Having a good chat

The first word of each sentence in this article has been left out. Fill in the missing words.

_____ a good chat may seem the easiest and most natural thing in the world. _____ is something we all do without thinking about it, most of the time. _____ really good conversations between two people don't happen too often.

_____ and think for a moment about all the people you know. _____ many of them are really good conversationalists? _____ are you like yourself? _____ people are good talkers. _____ can entertain. _____ can tell good stories. _____ can be the life and soul of the party. _____ they may not be good at two-way conversations. _____ will probably not be very good listeners; not really interested in what the other person has to say. _____ good listeners are people who pay attention; who listen carefully to what others say. _____ they don't always give much away about themselves.

_____ really good conversation is a two-way process, with give and take on both sides. _____ one person is talking, there are actually three conversations going on. _____ are the words being said aloud; there are the thoughts of the person listening and there are the thoughts of the person who is talking. _____ you are doing the talking, you can often tell if the other person is really interested. _____ they looking at you? _____ they fiddling with their hands, looking at their watch or shifting round in their seat? _____ may be able to hold their attention by not going on too long or by getting them to respond.

> _____ you have something important to communicate, follow these rules:
> - ❏ _____ the right person to talk to.
> - ❏ _____ sure the atmosphere is right - no TV or other noise in the background; no other people around to distract them.
> - ❏ _____ a moment when the person has time to listen and respond.
> - ❏ _____ possible, think beforehand about the best way of putting over what you want to say.
> - ❏ _____ the listener interested by letting them respond and by making sure that they understand what you are getting at.

Hero or villain ?

This is the beginning of a short romantic story. Read it, then do the exercises.

Emma arrived later than all the others on the training course. She had been late setting off and had got stuck in the rush hour traffic. She signed in at the desk and went through to the lounge where all the others were standing around, chatting and drinking coffee. She was aware that several people glanced in her direction as she made for the waitress standing behind the trolley with the coffee cups. She could feel herself begin to tense up as she failed to recognise anyone that she knew.

Collecting her coffee, she turned to face those awful first few moments, knowing that she would have to make conversation with total strangers. It was then that he turned his head and their eyes met. Her heart missed a beat. What on earth could he be doing here ?

She saw the smiling blue eyes, the thick dark hair and the bronzed skin that she remembered so well from the beach in Greece. He was wearing an expensive, beautifully cut suit with a silk tie. She could sense at once how the others with him were reacting to his charm and humour.

"Emma !" he said. "What a wonderful surprise ! Come and join us."

She felt her mouth go dry and her heart begin to pound. After all those weeks of trying to forget him, telling herself that she would never see him again. And now, there he was, standing next to her, smiling down at her ....

A. *What impression do you get of Emma from the story so far? Write a short character sketch of her.*

B. *Changing a few words in paragraph 3 could make the story completely different. Fill in the gaps in paragraph 3, given below, using words which describe the man as someone Emma remembers with fear and hatred.*

She saw the _____ eyes, the _____ hair and the _____ skin that she remembered so well from the _____ . He was wearing _____ suit with a _____ . She could sense at once how the others with him were reacting to his _____ and _____ .

C. *Finish the story in your own way, choosing **one** of the versions of paragraph 3. Give it a suitable title.*

Brown and Brown / *Finding the Words*

It can't be true (1)

A. *Fill in the gaps in these statements. All the missing words are short, everyday ones.*

1. The lead in an *HB* pencil will draw a line 35 miles _____ .

2. There _____ more types of beetle than of any other creature on earth.

3. Babies can breathe and swallow at the _____ time, but adults can't.

4. There isn't any soda _____ soda water.

5. Dogs sweat through _____ paws.

6. Birmingham has 22 more miles _____ canals than Venice.

7. An alsatian's sense of smell is a million times better _____ a human's.

8. An average human scalp _____ 100,000 hairs.

9. The British spend twice _____ much on pet food as on baby food.

10. On average, we lose 11oz *(312gm)* of weight _____ we are asleep at night.

B. *Which of the statements, do you think, are true and which are false?*

Answers to **B.** *on p.46*

Brown and Brown / *Finding the Words*

It can't be true (2)

A. Fill in the missing words in these statements.

1. Every day your heart pumps _____ blood to fill the fuel tanks of about 400 cars.

2. A West German firm makes artificial spray-on mud _____ owners of four-wheel-drive cars who live in cities but want their _____ to look as if they have been _____ in rough country.

3. William Shakespeare spelt _____ surname in 6 different ways. He _____ spelt it in 2 different ways in the same document.

4. The horn of the rhinoceros is not a bone. It is, in fact, _____ hair.

5. Office _____ in London is now so expensive that it _____ £50 a year to rent the space taken up _____ an average wastepaper basket.

6. More women than men try to commit suicide but more men succeed in their _____ .

7. The first international cricket _____ in the world was played in 1844. It was _____ the U.S.A. and Canada !

8. In Finland, there are no widely _____ swear words, so they adopted the word *ravintolassa*. Translated into _____ , it means *in the restaurant* !

9. The only food _____ by a German nun in thirty-five years was the _____ wafer taken at morning mass.

10. The screwdriver was invented _____ the screw. It was originally used to _____ bent nails.

B. Which of the statements, do you think, are true and which are false ?

*Answers to **B**. on p.46*

Brown and Brown / Finding the Words

My Best Shot

An eighteen-year-old soccer player with a Second Division side has just been bought for £1.5 million by a Premier League club. He gives an interview to the local newspaper after a few days at his new club.

Write down what the footballer says in the interview, using at least 10 of the phrases given in the box below.

- over the moon
- a much higher work-rate
- one of the lads
- raising my game
- out in the sticks
- getting quality ball
- out of the blue
- joining the big time
- moving up a gear
- a harsh fitness regime
- at the end of the day
- sick as a parrot
- on the park
- the danger zone
- in a different league
- when it comes down to it

On tap

A. Fill in the gaps in this article. All the missing words are nouns.

What is the most valuable resource in the world ? Ask the average person in Western _____ or North America this question and they are likely to say that it is gold or _____, oil, coal or natural gas. In fact, the most vital and precious _____ of all is water.

We take it for granted that we can turn on a _____ and get clean water. We get angry when water _____ ask us to cut down our _____ of water and object to or ignore _____ on the use of hosepipes and car _____. Each year, we use more and more water. Every _____ of water we use requires _____ to clean it, to pump it to our _____ and then to clean it again before it is returned to the _____ or the sea.

In other parts of the _____, water is never taken for granted. Millions of poor _____ have to fetch and carry all the water they need. In many _____, the only water people can get is not clean and carries _____. In a country such as Bangladesh, every _____ could lose two children in infancy and one _____ in every five dies before it is a year old. Many of these _____ are from water-related diseases.

Experts have said that, by the _____ 2025, about two-thirds of the world's _____ could be short of clean water. _____ could easily break out over _____ of water in places where one large river - the River Nile in North _____, for example - passes through several countries.

Saving water makes sense for _____, wherever they live. It is time that water was treated with the _____ it deserves. After all, life on this _____ depends on it.

B. What do you think?

Write down or discuss answers to the questions below.

1. Where does the water in your area come from, where is it stored and where is it treated ?
2. How could your family reduce its use of water ?
3. What does the phrase '**on tap**' mean and where do you think it comes from ?

Out for a duck

Choose a word from the box to fill each of the gaps in the story.

coming	lighting	making	sinking
fearing	seeing	digging	grabbing
running	hunting	seeking	killing
looking	finding	thinking	going
contacting	passing	using	shooting

A man in North America had just bought a brand new Jeep Cherokee. He and a friend decided to enjoy a day out in it, _____ duck with his black labrador. _____ that all the lakes were frozen solid, they drove out on to the ice. They decided that _____ a large hole in the ice would be a good way to attract any _____ ducks _____ for fish. Instead of _____ a pick-axe or a drill, they chose to use dynamite.

They thought that it would be too risky to plant the dynamite and run off after _____ the fuse, as they might slip on the ice. Instead, they simply lit the 40-second fuse and threw it as far as they possibly could. Unfortunately, the labrador, _____ that the fun had begun, set off after the dynamite. _____ the dynamite in its mouth, it ran straight back towards the men. They shouted and screamed but the dog kept _____ . _____ death, one of them let fly with his shotgun.

Buckshot is not too good at _____ an animal as big as a labrador and the injured dog ran to take cover under the brand new Jeep. Seconds later, the dog, the dynamite and over £30,000-worth of Cherokee blew up and sank to the bottom of the lake. The owner, on _____ his insurance company, was told that his policy did not cover _____ a vehicle by the illegal use of explosives!

Race of a lifetime

A.   Choose phrases from the box to fill the gaps in this story.

like a rocket	nothing left in her legs	pick off
boxed in	out of her skin	stand a chance
stay in touch	on her shoulder	a photo finish
Go for it!	Phew! What a scorcher!	claw its way back
went up a gear	a final dash	the last lap
lost it	an outside chance	all hell broke loose
as long as	hang in	the last chance

It was the final of the 1500 metres for women. It had been a boiling hot day in Athens and now, even at eight o'clock in the evening, the heat was almost unbearable. Josie could already see tomorrow's newspaper headline: " _____ "

Josie knew that she had _____ of a medal, but only if she ran _____ . She had a really fast finish and, to make good use of it, she needed to _____ with the leading pack for the first couple of laps. _____ the race was not too quick in the early stages, she should be able to pace herself and _____ there.

She was surprised when the Russian shot off _____ at the starting gun, while the rest of the field held back. Then, gradually, the pack began to _____ to the leader and by the end of the second lap the Russian was being overhauled.

Josie was lying in ninth place and wasn't feeling too drained, despite the heat. Slowly she began to _____ the runners in front of her. At the bell for the last lap she was in third place but, unfortunately, she was _____ on the inside. Unless she could make a space for herself and edge out, she wouldn't _____ .

On the final bend..............

B.   Finish the story, including phrases from the box which have not yet been used.

Brown and Brown / Finding the Words

Reading Instructions (1)

1. *The first word of each instruction for recording is missing. Fit each of the words from the box into one of the gaps.*

STEREO RADIO CASSETTE RECORDER

Recording Radio Broadcasts

1. _____ Function Selector to "RADIO".

2. _____ Band Selector to desired radio band.

3. _____ in your favourite station using Tuning Control.

4. _____ Volume and Tone Controls.

5. _____ cassette tape into right-hand Cassette Compartment

6. _____ Record Button.

7. _____ stop recording, press Stop/Eject Button.

8. _____ Function Selector to "TAPE/OFF" to turn unit off.

| Tune | Set | Press | Adjust |
| Set | To | Insert | Set |

2. a. Look quickly through the recording instructions and estimate roughly how many capital letters they contain.

b. Read carefully through the recording instructions and write down the exact number of capital letters they contain. How close were your estimate and the exact number ?

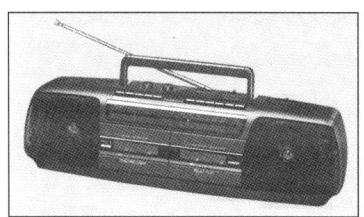

Reading Instructions (2)

A. *Choose a word from the box to fill each gap in the freezer instructions.*

UPRIGHT FREEZER

How to de-frost

Larger accumulations of ice or _____ in the freezing trays impede the _____ of the appliance and increase energy _____ . About 4 hours before de-frosting switch on the super-freeze to ensure that the _____ is thoroughly frozen. Then remove the freezing baskets containing the _____ and place the artificial ice-blocks directly on top of the food. Wrap the baskets in several _____ of newspaper or in a blanket and keep in a cool _____ .

Leave the door of the freezer open and disconnect _____ from mains. Empty the top frozen food _____ and place it directly under the drainage _____ *(Fig 1, No.12)* to collect the thaw water. Try to defrost the _____ as quickly as possible. Clean the _____ of the freezer thoroughly after defrosting.

Fig. 1

appliance	bin	consumption	products
food	interior	place	hoar-frost
efficiency	unit	outlet	layers

B. *All the words in the box are of one kind. What are they?*

C. *Instructions are often written in a shortened form in which unimportant words are left out.*

    e.g. **Place the freezer in a cool corner of the kitchen out of the sun.** *(Full version)*
         Place freezer in cool corner of kitchen out of sun. *(Shortened version)*

Re-write the freezer instructions, leaving out words which you think are unimportant.

Reading Instructions (3)

Read the instructions for recharging the shaver, then do the exercises below.

ELECTRIC SHAVER

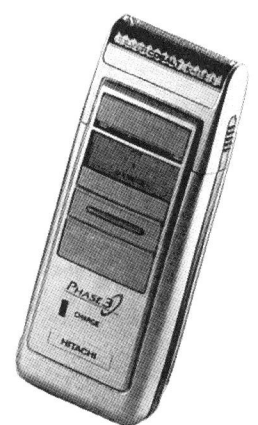

Recharging your shaver

This shaver is fitted with a quick charge facility that will enable batteries to be recharged to 85% capacity in one hour.

To fully charge the shaver allow it to be recharged overnight *(8 hours)*. The energy consumption for recharging is minimal and the cells cannot be overcharged.

Periodically *(every 6 months)* the shaver should be totally discharged during normal use and then fully recharged for the eight hour period. This will prolong the life of the cells and give a better shaving performance.

1. a. Make a list of all the words in the shaver instructions which have the word '**charge**' as their root word.

    b. Can you think of any other words which have '**charge**' as their root word?

2. Each of these words from the shaver instructions has several shades of meaning. Put each word into a sentence which uses it in a different way from the one in the instructions.

overcharged	quick	performance
cells	fitted	consumption

3. Re-read paragraph 3 of the shaver instructions. What exactly does it mean? Can you think of any problems that might arise when following this instruction?

Reading Instructions (4)

Read the instructions for the cordless jug kettle, then do the exercises.

CORDLESS JUG KETTLE

Use kettle only with power base supplied and vice versa.

Ensure that kettle is properly located on power base before switching it on.

Close lid before using kettle, otherwise it may switch off.

Do not open lid while water is being heated.

Remove kettle from its power base before filling or pouring.

Do not attempt to remove kettle from its power base until it is switched off, either manually or automatically.

In use

When filling or carrying kettle, do not tilt it backwards, as this may allow water to pass through steam aperture on to control area. Should this occur, kettle must be allowed to dry before use.

Pour slowly to avoid the risk of splashing.

1. *Give another word or phrase which could be used instead of each of these words from the instructions:*

    supplied   **ensure**   **located**   **aperture**   **occur**

2. *Explain what '**vice versa**' means in the first sentence of the instructions.*

3. *The instructions are written in a short form in which the word '**the**' is left out. Re-write the instructions, putting in '**the**' where it is missing.*

Reading Instructions (5)

Read the instructions for storing numbers, then do the exercises.

TELEPHONE

Storing numbers in memory

There are two ways of storing numbers in the memory: a one-touch system which allows you to store three numbers, and a two-touch system which allows you to store an additional ten numbers. Each memory location can store up to 16 digits.

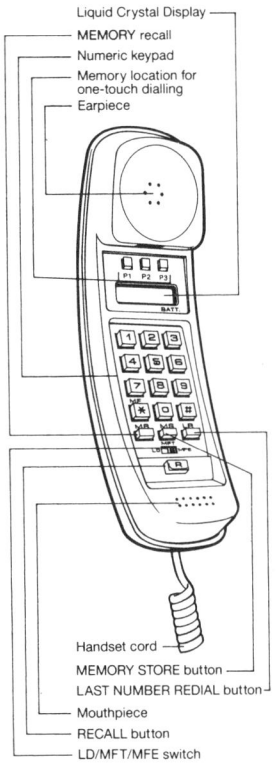

One-touch memory location

Lift the handset

press MS

key the number

press a memory button (P1, P2 or P3)

Two-touch memory location

Lift the handset

press MS

key the number

press MS

press a keypad button (0 to 9) to select a memory location

Don't forget to fill in the memory index card after storing a number.

Using a Dictionary

1. *Look up these words from the instructions in a standard dictionary, then explain what they mean in your own words.*

   system   **digits**   **index**

2. *a. Look up the meaning and origin of each of these words from the instructions:*

   location   **memory**

   b. Add prefixes and / or suffixes to the root of each of the above words to make new ones. Put each of the new words into a sentence which explains its meaning.

   e.g.   ***mem**orise*   *dis**loc**ated*

Reading Instructions (6)

A. *Fill in the gaps in the Power Shower instructions. All the missing words are verbs.*

POWER SHOWER

Maintenance

Periodic cleaning of the strainer will be required.
This can be _____ as follows:

1. _____ the flexible hose from the handset (see Fig. 1).

2. _____ and clean the strainer.

3. _____ the strainer and re-assemble.

Fig. 1 — Handset, Strainer, Hose

To _____ the spray performance, the spray plate must be kept clean.

To _____ the spray plate holes:

1. _____ the handset into a proprietary descaling solution, following manufacturer's instructions.

2. Rinse and _____ to hose, ensuring strainer is in position.

Fig. 2 — Handset, Seal, Adaptor, Strainer, Hose

B. *Think of at least 5 verbs, apart from the ones in the instructions, which begin with* **'re-'**.

Reading Instructions (7)

1. Choose a word from the box to fill each gap in the instructions.

DIGITAL WATCH

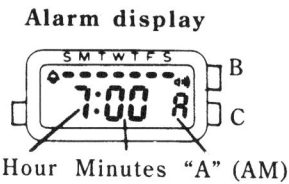

Alarm display

Hour Minutes "A" (AM)

How to stop the alarm

The alarm rings at the _____ time for 30 seconds and stops. _____ , the alarm can be stopped _____ by depressing button **C** in any display.

Alarm Test

The alarm can be _____ with a beeping sound by _____ buttons **B** and **C** at the same time in the time/calendar _____ .

tested	depressing	manually
designated	display	however

2. Think of another word (or words) which could replace each of the words in the box.

3. Each of these words from the instructions above has several shades of meaning. Put each word into a sentence which uses it in a different way from the one in the instructions.

    depressing   stops   seconds

    display   alarm   sound

Safe and sound

Every tenth word has been left out of this article. Fill in the missing words.

In the U.K., at least one home is broken _____ every minute, according to police figures. This figure could _____ to almost two every minute if the unreported burglaries _____ the failed attempts were included. However, it is not _____ doom and gloom. Most burglars are on the lookout _____ easy pickings and a few simple measures may persuade _____ to try elsewhere.

- **LOCK UP**   It may seem obvious, _____ make sure that you lock doors and windows when _____ go out - even if it's only for a short _____ . One in five burglars gets in through an unlocked _____ or window. Burglaries even happen when people are at _____ , so close doors and windows which could tempt a _____ to try his luck.

- **IMPROVE YOUR LOCKS**   All outer _____ should have 5-lever or 7-lever mortise locks, with an _____ cylinder lock fitted on the front door. Back doors _____ have bolts as well as locks, and patio doors _____ have special locks with bolts top and bottom. All _____ floor windows and accessible upstairs windows should have window _____ *(but make sure that keys for them are easily _____ inside the house, in case of fire).*

- **LIGHTS**   Although _____ half of all burglaries happen at night, it is _____ to leave lights on and curtains drawn if you _____ out when it is dark. Lights, TV and radio _____ be turned on and off by timers. External lights _____ put off burglars.

- **DON'T MAKE IT EASY**   Never leave _____ tools, ladders etc. lying around. Keep them in a _____ shed or indoors. Don't leave valuables on display in _____ house. Hide small valuable items in unusual places *(don't _____ a valuable gold ring in a jewellery box in _____ bedroom).* Join a *Neighbourhood Watch* scheme, if you can.

- **_____ YOUR PROPERTY**   Basic household contents insurance doesn't have to _____ all that much and it gives you some peace _____ mind. Many of the items most often stolen *(videos, _____ , hi-fi, cameras)* are easily replaced but, remember, you may _____ to pay the first £50 or £100 of any _____ .

- **ALARMS**   Burglar alarms and sensors can deter burglars but _____ may be expensive to install and maintain. Take the _____ measures detailed first.

Signs and Notices (1)

There is one mistake in each of these signs and notices. What is it?

①

In case of fire break grass for key

②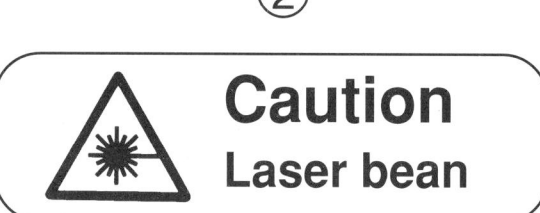

③

④

Not for us on electrical fires

⑤

Signs and Notices (2)

There is one mistake in each of these signs and notices. What is it?

①

Private property
Keep in

②

Reversed parking

③

Thieves will be prostituted

④

All visitor must report to reception

⑤

Representatives see only by appointment

Signs and Notices (3)

There is one mistake in each of these signs and notices. What is it?

①  No unauthorised person allowed beyond this pint

②  Caution
In the even of fire do not use this lift

③ Automatic fine door keep clear Close at night

④  Do not wear loos clothing when operating this machine

⑤ This door to be secured open went the premises are occupied

Signs and Notices (4)

There is one mistake in each of these signs and notices. What is it?

①

To be used only in the event off fire

②

Cheques can only be accepted if supporter by a cheque card

③

Users of this car park do so at their own risk and the management carrot accept liability for accident, loss or damage

④

No dogs allowed except on a leach

⑤

Smoking or naked lights positively forbid beyond this point

⑥

It is the responsibility of the diver to ensure that passengers do not travel on this vehicle

That takes the biscuit!

Fill in the missing words in this story.

An elderly woman went into a café one morning. She bought a _____ of coffee and a packet of biscuits at the counter. The _____ was quite full and the only spare seat was at a table for _____, where a man sat alone.

The man was _____-looking and unshaven. She asked him if the chair opposite was _____ and he grunted back at her and _____ his head.

After a minute or two, she _____ up the packet of biscuits from the table, opened it and took one out. _____, the man leant across and also took a biscuit from the packet. She _____ that she should say something but she was a bit _____ of the man and thought he might become _____. She decided to say nothing.

In a little while, she _____ another biscuit. To her surprise, the man again leant _____ and took one for himself. The woman thought of _____ to the owner of the café but, once more, she decided to keep _____.

Finally, the man leant across and took the _____ biscuit. He broke it in half and, with a grin, _____ her one half. He then finished his coffee, got up and _____, leaving the old woman quite upset and shaken. _____ she had calmed down a bit, she got up to leave. As she did so, a packet of _____ fell off her lap on to the floor.

The Blizzard

Fill in the missing parts of this story.

It was the middle of January. The farm was only a few miles from Snowdon, on the western slope of the valley. It was seven in the morning when the snow began to fall, very gently. The sheep had to be fed and brought down nearer to the farm buildings. Gwyn loaded up the trailer before setting off ....

Soon after 11 o'clock, the wind began to pick up. The snow was falling heavily by then ....

By 3.30, it was already quite dark. The snow lay thick everywhere and the wind continued to pile it up in deep drifts wherever anything got in its way ....

The Day of the Exam

Fill in the missing parts of this story.

I had been preparing for the day of the exam for weeks. I had worked really hard at getting all my coursework up to date and I had spent a lot of time revising. I hate exams. I get all worked up and nervous beforehand and I need to be well prepared and calm if I am to do at all well.

Anyway, that Tuesday morning, I set off on my bike at 9 o'clock. The exam didn't start until 10 a.m., so I had plenty of time ....

Eventually, I got there at five minutes past ten. I had to go into that big hall, with 50 people already scribbling away in complete silence ....

The results were announced three weeks later. I could hardly bring myself to go and look at the noticeboard ....

The Great Canadian Ice Storm

Fill in the gaps in this news story.
All the missing words are verbs.

An ice storm happens when warm moist air meets very cold air from the polar regions. The moist air _____ as super-cooled rain which freezes on contact with whatever it touches. Ice storms _____ quite often in Canada, perhaps two or three times each winter. Usually a storm _____ for a few hours and doesn't _____ too much damage.

Broken electricity pylons

On the night of January 6th, 1998, an ice storm _____ in Eastern Ontario and went on and on and on. The freezing rain _____ for several days and nights, causing an incredible amount of damage. Tree branches became _____ in shells of ice an inch thick and the trees couldn't support the weight. Branches _____ to the ground, crushing cars and the roofs of buildings. Power pylons supporting high tension wires _____ like matchsticks. Electricity cables sagged lower and lower with the weight of ice and then _____ .

When the ice storms stopped, a new danger _____ . As the temperature rose a little, huge blocks of ice weighing up to 20 kilograms _____ to fall from trees, pylons and buildings. Yet more damage was caused to buildings, vehicles and animals. Anyone who _____ outside their home risked injury or even death, but staying indoors _____ neither safe nor pleasant.

People were _____ in their homes without power, without telephones or any other form of communication. 25 people _____ . Some died of hypothermia because their central heating systems _____ useless without electricity for the pump and ignition. Others were _____ by carbon monoxide from oil and gas heaters _____ indoors without ventilation.

A major disaster such as this one _____ the headlines for a week or two but, long after the newspapers have _____ interest, the real effects remain - the businesses in ruins, the homes to be _____ and the lives to be rebuilt in the hope that such a terrifying event will never, ever, _____ again.

Brown and Brown / Finding the Words

41

The Modern Wedding

The last word of each sentence in this article is missing.
Choose a word from the box to fill each gap.

These days, more marriages end in divorce and many don't last longer than a year or _____ . Despite this, weddings seem to get more and more expensive and elaborate in _____ . Couples (or their parents!) usually spend several thousand pounds on their 'big day', and sums of £10,000 are not _____ .

An Alaskan Wedding

Traditional religious ceremonies are still popular, even though fewer young people regularly attend a place of _____ . Many couples continue to get married in a registry office but, since the change in the law, it seems that marriages can now take place almost _____ . Public buildings, country houses and hotels can all be registered for _____ . Hotels are beginning to offer 'wedding packages' in which they organise the ceremony, the reception, an evening dance and accommodation for all the _____ .

Quite a lot of couples now go abroad for their _____ . The West Indies, the Dominican Republic, Mexico and countries in the Far East are all popular except, perhaps, with the parents, bridesmaids and best man if they have to pay their own _____ !

There is also a fashion for unusual weddings, especially in _____ . Some couples have been known to get married in the nude or under _____ . Others have tied the knot while flying in aeroplanes or hang- _____ . Sky-diving, driving at high speed and riding on roller coasters are even crazier _____ .

Whether any of these ceremonies makes any difference to the length of time that the marriage lasts is not _____ .

choices	design	recorded	water
friends	uncommon	so	America
wedding	ground	marriages	way
two	honeymoon	guests	worship
unusual	known	gliders	ideas
Australia	style	anywhere	expenses

The Sad Tale of Mr. Goodyear

Read the story, then do the exercises below.

Goodyear is one of the world's best-known brand names for car tyres. The story of Charles Goodyear, after whom the company is named, is not so well known.

Charles Goodyear was an American inventor in the 19th Century. In 1834, he became very interested in rubber. At that time, the pure rubber obtained from rubber trees did not have many uses. Although it was flexible, waterproof and tough when it was cold, rubber could not stand up to heat. In hot weather, it melted and began to smell. Goodyear thought he ought to be able to get round the problem but he had no idea how to do it.

Over the next 9 years, he spent every penny (or dime!) he had on his experiments. He borrowed money from his friends and relatives and turned the kitchen of his home into a laboratory. He nearly killed himself and his family several times. Nothing that he tried worked. He borrowed $46,000 from his brother-in-law but all the money went on useless experiments. His family was so poor that, in 1840, when his 2-year-old son died, they couldn't afford a coffin.

Finally, in 1843, he made his breakthrough. By accident, he spilt some India rubber and sulphur on top of his stove. This mixture created a flexible and adaptable material that withstood heat and cold, and it didn't smell. He had invented the substance known as 'vulcanised rubber'. He formed a company *(N.I.R. Co.)* to make it and he took out patents to protect his invention.

Unfortunately, the method of production was so simple that other manufacturers just stole the idea. Goodyear took up the matter in court, but without success. The French gave him a patent and then withdrew it. He went to France to complain and was thrown into prison. When Goodyear died in 1860, his family was left with huge debts.

So where do *Goodyear* tyres come from? Two brothers in a town in Ohio set up the company and named it after Goodyear just because they admired his invention.

A. *Find a word in the story which means the same as each of these words.*

    strong   **cash**   **easy**   **gaol**   **discovered**   **enormous**

B. *Find a word in the story which means the opposite of each of these words.*

    saved   **lent**   **enemies**   **destroyed**   **despised**   **failure**

C. *Look up these words in a dictionary, then explain what they mean in your own words:*

    flexible   **patent**   **adaptable**   **vulcanised**   **dime**

The War-time Volunteer

The last word in each sentence of this story is missing.
Think of a suitable word to fill each gap.

Michael Bentine, the comedian, who died in 1996, often told this story about his time as an air-raid volunteer during the _____ .

He was put in charge of a young ambulance team of himself and two other _____ . One day, as part of an exercise, they were asked to find a volunteer who would act as a casualty so that the ambulance team and the hospital could practise dealing with an _____ .

That morning, the sea-front at Folkestone was deserted but, after a while, an elderly retired naval officer came walking along the cliff _____ . The team went up to him and asked if he would be their _____ . He _____ . They got him to lie down on the stretcher and they put bandages and splints on him as if he was a real _____ .

Michael Bentine then went to the head of the stretcher to lift it _____ . As he nodded to his colleague to lift the other end, his tin helmet fell _____ . It hit the old man on the head like a guillotine and knocked him out _____ . In a panic, the team picked up the stretcher and shoved it into the back of the ambulance as fast as they _____ . In doing so, they jammed two of the old man's fingers in the _____ . They then found that the stretcher was too long for the ambulance and they couldn't close the back _____ .

Bentine thought of a _____ . He took off his tie and knotted it through the handles of the half-closed _____ . He then rang the hospital to say that they were bringing in a real casualty who had head _____ . The old ambulance was difficult to start but, when it did get going, they shot off at high _____ . As they went round the first corner, at Earls Avenue, the tie _____ . Stretcher and casualty shot out of the open doors and crashed to the _____ .

Amazingly, the old man recovered from his _____ . He didn't seem to blame the lads for what had _____ . He took the line that it could have happened to _____ .

World Records

Choose a word from the box to fill each of the gaps in the questions below, then try to answer the questions.

| heaviest | largest | many | far | tallest | fastest |
| lightest | shortest | greatest | longest | biggest | long |

1. How _____ has someone walked with a milk bottle balanced on his head ?

2. How _____ has someone stayed balanced on one leg ?

3. How _____ yards of spaghetti were eaten in 12.02 seconds in Halesowen in 1986 ?

4. What is the _____ amount of money raised by a charity walk ?

5. What is the _____ single unbroken apple peel ever peeled ?

6. What is the _____ weight ever lifted by someone with his teeth ?

7. What is the _____ that a man has ever grown ?

8. What is the _____ number of couples to have kissed at the same time in the same place ?

9. What is the weight of the _____ leek ever grown in the world ?

10. What is the _____ that anyone has walked 50 metres on their hands ?

11. What is weight of the _____ surviving baby ever born in the U.K. ?

12. What is the _____ time taken by two nurses to make a hospital bed ?

World Records Answers on p.47

Brown and Brown / Finding the Words

Words omitted from the texts

The words missing from 'cloze' and other exercises are given below, under their page numbers, in the order they appear in the text.

*Answers to the questions asked in **It can't be true (1) & (2)** (pp. 20 & 21) and in **World Records** (p.45) are given below under their page numbers.*

4. *A Breath of Fresh Air:* entirely, bustle, overpowered, live, their, window, for, silence, football, pollution, Most, buffer, areas, there, as, housing, go, not, actually, where

5. *A Deaf Ear (1):* deaf, years, new, asked, ear, found, inside, said, put

8. *Beware of pickpockets:* warned, try, stuck, got, remembered, gone, close, closed, pull, forced, held, sped, had, arrived, could, wanted, said, know, went

9. *Blackpool Pleasure Beach:* out of this world; young at heart; something for everyone; got the bottle; biggest and best; stomach-churning; anything for a quiet life; a bird's eye view; romance is in the air; seen it all before; thrills and spills; soaked to the skin; a bite to eat; To crown it all; the holiday of a lifetime

10. *Come up and see me:* men, bad, White, tried, worth, over, but, ready

11. *Crimes that went wrong (1):* out, by, who, to, and, over, the, off, a, Her, with, in

12. *Crimes that went wrong (2):* group, night, business, they, door, money, wall, seconds, walls, rubble, thing, safe

13. *Dropping a line (1):* 1. letter 2. find 3. inform 4. sorry 5. apologise 6. confidential 7. attending 8. reply

14. *Dropping a line (2):* 1. selected, draw 2. queries, reference 3. copy, hearing 4. renew, possible 5. kind, accept 6. due, write 7. regrets, requests 8. rate, circulation

15. *Food scares:* last, been, a, Cases, was, were, serious, resulted, Other, fruit, milk, been, no, to, to, there, changes, still, risk, cuts, beef, was, U.K., and, same, the, food, is, do, that, what, answer, cut, in, be, kept, it, around, the, fruit, carbohydrate, foods

18. *Having a good chat:* Having, Talking, But, Stop, How, What, Some, They, They, They, But, They, The, But, A, When, There, When, Are, Are, You, If, Pick, Make, Choose, If, Keep

20. *It can't be true (1):* **A.** 1. long 2. are 3. same 4. in 5. their 6. of 7. than 8. has 9. as 10. while **B.** All the statements are true

21. *It can't be true (2):* **A.** 1. enough 2. for, cars, used 3. his, even 4. its 5. space, costs, by 6. attempts 7. match, between 8. used, English 9. eaten, holy 10. before, extract **B.** All the statements are true.

23. *On tap* Europe, silver, thing, tap, companies, use, bans, washes, drop, energy, homes, river, world, people, countries, disease, mother, baby, deaths, year, population, wars, sources, Africa, everyone, care, planet

24. *Out for a duck:* shooting, Seeing, making, passing, looking, using, lighting, thinking, Grabbing, coming, Fearing, killing, contacting, sinking

25. *Race of a lifetime:* Phew! What a scorcher!; an outside chance; out of her skin; stay in touch; As long as; hang in; like a rocket; claw its way back; pick off; boxed in; stand a chance

26. *Reading Instructions (1):* 1. Set 2. Set 3. Tune 4. Adjust 5. Insert 6. Press 7. To 8. Set

27. *Reading Instructions (2):* hoar-frost, efficiency, consumption, food, products, layers, place, appliance, bin, outlet, unit, interior   B. All the words are nouns.

31. *Reading Instructions (6):* achieved, Remove, Remove, refit, maintain, clean, Dip, re-assemble

32. *Reading Instructions (7):* designated, However, manually, tested, depressing, display

33. *Safe and sound:* into, increase, and, all, for, them, but, you, time, door, home, thief, doors, extra, should, should, ground, locks, available, only, wise, are, can, often, garden, locked, the, leave, the, Insure, cost, of, TVs, have, claim, they, other

34. *Signs and Notices (1):* 1. In case of fire break **glass** for key   2. Caution Laser **beam** 3. No tipping or **dumping**   4. <u>Not</u> for **use** on electrical fires   5. **Warning** Dust hazard

35. *Signs and Notices (2):* 1. Private property Keep **out**   2. **Reserved** parking 3. Thieves will be **prosecuted**   4. All **visitors** must report to reception 5. Representatives **seen** only by appointment

36. *Signs and Notices (3):* 1. No unauthorised person allowed beyond this **point** 2. Caution In the **event** of fire do not use this lift   3. Automatic **fire** door keep clear Close at night   4. Do not wear **loose** clothing when operating this machine 5. This door to be secured open **when** the premises are occupied

37. *Signs and Notices (4):* 1. To be used only in the event **of** fire   2. Cheques can only be accepted if **supported** by a cheque card   3. Users of this car park do so at their own risk and the management **cannot** accept liability for accident, loss or damage 4. No dogs allowed except on a **leash**   5. Smoking or naked lights positively **forbidden** beyond this point   6. It is the responsibility of the **driver** to ensure that passengers do not travel on this vehicle

38. *That takes the biscuit!:* cup, café, two, rough, empty, nodded, picked, Suddenly, knew, scared, abusive, took, across, going, quiet, last, gave, went, After, biscuits

41. *The Great Canadian Ice Storm:* falls, occur, lasts, cause, started, fell, coated, crashed, snapped, broke, emerged, began, ventured, was, trapped, died, were, poisoned, used, grabs, lost, repaired, happen

42. *The Modern Wedding:* so, style, uncommon, worship, anywhere, marriages, guests, wedding, way, America, water, gliders, choices, recorded

44. *The War-time Volunteer:* war, teenagers, emergency, tops, volunteer, agreed, casualty, up, off, cold, could, runners, doors, solution, doors, injuries, speed, snapped, ground, injuries, happened, anyone

45. *World Records:* 1. far; *70 miles 282 yds / 113.8 km (1993)*   2. long; *71 hours 40 mins (1995)* 3. many; *100 yards / 91.4m (1986)*   4. largest; *£9.1 million (1980)* 5. longest; *52.51m / 172ft 4in (1976)*   6. heaviest; *281.5kg / 620lb 10oz (1990)* 7. tallest; *8ft 11¹/₁₀ in / 2.72m (1918-1940)*   8. greatest; *1420 (1996)* 9. biggest; *5.5kg / 12lb 2oz (1987)*   10. fastest; *16.93 seconds (1994)* 11. lightest; *283g / 10oz (1938)*   12. shortest; *14 seconds (1993)*

Index

Exercises

Choosing phrases from a box *(exact no. given)*	9
Choosing phrases from a box *(multiple choice)*	22,25
Choosing words from a box *(exact no. given)*	5,11,13,26,27,32,45
Choosing words from a box *(multiple choice)*	4,24,42
Cloze exercises:	
- *first words*	18
- *general*	10,14,15,20,21,33,38
- *last words*	44
- *nouns*	12,23
- *verbs*	8,31,41
Finishing a story	19,25,39,40
Free writing	7,17,19,22,23,25,39,40
Guessing answers	20,21,45
Instructions *(abbreviating & expanding)*	27,29
Nouns	12,23,27
Sentence completion	16,19
Skimming / Scanning	7,8,12,17,26,28,29,43
True/False questions	20,21
Using phrases in writing	16,22,25
Verbs	8,31,41
Vocabulary:	
- *finding the error*	34-37
- *root words / prefixes / suffixes*	28,30
- *thinking of alternatives to given words*	6,7,13,17,19,29,31,32,43
- *using a word too often*	7,17
- *word meanings / using a dictionary*	28,29,30,32,43

Topics

Biographical	10,17,40,43,44
Countryside	4,16,24
Crime	8,11,12,33
Fictional stories	17,19,25,39,40
Food / Eating	7,15,38
Humour	5,6,8,10,11,12,24,38,44
Instructions	26-32
Issues	4,15,16,17,23,33
Leisure / Home	7,9,17,42
Letter writing	13,14
News items	11,12,41,42,43
Relationships / Communication	18,19,42
Signs & Notices	34-37
Sport	22,25
Unusual facts & Records	20,21,45